Bibliografische Information der Deutschen Nationalbibliothek:

Die Deutsche Bibliothek verzeichnet diese Publikation in der Deutschen National-
bibliografie; detaillierte bibliografische Daten sind im Internet über http://dnb.d-
nb.de/ abrufbar.

Impressum:

Copyright © 2009 GRIN Verlag, Open Publishing GmbH
Druck und Bindung: Books on Demand GmbH, Norderstedt Germany
ISBN: 9783640619955

Dieses Buch bei GRIN:

http://www.grin.com/de/e-book/150471/the-pros-and-cons-of-currency-unions

Anna Lena Rembrecht

The pros and cons of currency unions

GRIN Verlag

GRIN - Your knowledge has value

Der GRIN Verlag publiziert seit 1998 wissenschaftliche Arbeiten von Studenten, Hochschullehrern und anderen Akademikern als eBook und gedrucktes Buch. Die Verlagswebsite www.grin.com ist die ideale Plattform zur Veröffentlichung von Hausarbeiten, Abschlussarbeiten, wissenschaftlichen Aufsätzen, Dissertationen und Fachbüchern.

Besuchen Sie uns im Internet:

http://www.grin.com/

http://www.facebook.com/grincom

http://www.twitter.com/grin_com

Lehrstuhl für Theoretische Volkswirtschaftslehre I

Ruhr-Universität-Bochum
Fakultät für Wirtschaftswissenschaften

The pros and cons of currency union:
A Reserve Bank perspective

Based on an address by Donald T. Brash,
Governor of the Reserve Bank of New Zealand,
22 May 2000

Seminar in monetary policy WT 09/10

Filing date: November 10, 2009

Contents

1. Introduction.. p. 1

1.1 Digression:

Some myths about the currency union...p. 2

2. Advantages of the currency union..p. 2

3. Disadvantages of the currency union.. p. 3

3.1 Digression:

The Taylor rule and its relevance to New Zealand monetary policy..................... p. 4

4. Conclusion...p. 5

5. List of literature ....p. 7

Introduction

The creation of the monetary union in Europe, and also the interest of some Latin American countries to adopt the U.S. dollar in the year 1999 have provoked some interest in whether entering a currency union might also be an appropriate policy direction for New Zealand, or whether New Zealand should keep its own freely floating currency. Donald T. Brash, governor of the reserve bank of New Zealand, analyzed the advantages and disadvantages of a new currency system in New Zealand in his address to the Auckland Rotary Club in 2000. Brash indicates that every decision to change a currency system has a political dimension and we have to consider, that this means the integration of the whole state in a new legal, trade and political system. And it seems very clear from the European experience, the step to monetary union is not just an economic one, it is inherently a political one. When we have to evaluate the benefits or the disadvantages of new ways in currency politics, we have to consider that this is also a foreign policy decision. Brash calls two different opportunities to introduce a new currency system in New Zealand. He emphasizes the difference between *"currency union"* and *"dollarization"* (Brash, 2000, p.74). Currency union means to launch a new central bank for both countries and a new currency. The best example is the European Union with the creation of the ECB as the leading currency institution in Europe. The other possibility, Brash calls, is the simple adoption of an established currency like the U.S. dollar or the Australian dollar. The accent of Brash's analyses is the consideration of the currency union.

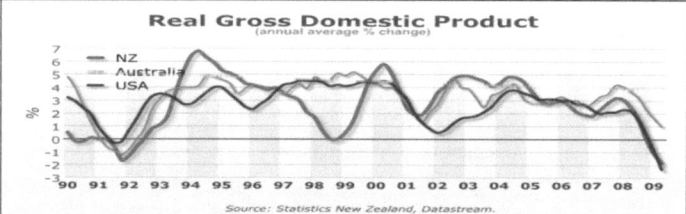

For a clear assessment, New Zealand's GDP growth rate compared with its two largest trading partners Australia and the USA.

The following argumentation refers to the study of two scientists, Holmes and Grimes, "An ANZAC Dollar?" Especially the option to cooperate with Australia was pursuant to a study of two economists, Sir Frank Holmes and Dr. Arthur Grimes. By diversifying against a broader range of shocks, a link to a larger currency area may result in a beneficial regime change.

Businesses are strongly of that opinion and there is little economic evidence to the contrary. A link to a larger currency may additional encourage new firms to locate in New Zealand to service the broader market. It may also enable existing New Zealand firms to expand into exporting where that is currently perceived as being too risky as a result of exchange rate volatility. Advantages, especially through joining a USD-based bloc, could also accrue through reductions in funding costs. Given these factors, and the overwhelmingly supportive views of business, the option of adopting a common currency area with the AUD or the USD must be taken seriously by all those who seek to boost conditions for economic development within New Zealand. So the microeconomic aspects of this study focuses on transaction costs, exchange rate risk and their impact on trade and investment. Their survey results indicate that New Zealand business, especially small or medium size firms, are favourably disposed towards an Australia-New Zealand monetary union. Brash points out, that in any case of adopting the Australian monetary system as a common currency, New Zealand would relinquish their influence to the decisions considering the monetary policy. Brash stresses, an important aspect is not to loose the influence to the monetary economic decisions. In the case of the United States the only possibility would be the takeover of the U.S. dollar, but New Zealand would never be influential to affect economic policy of large countries such as the United States.

Digression: Brash calls some myths about the currency union, which should be considered before giving a statement. First of all, the possible abolishment of the Reserve Bank would influence the banker's arguments to not create a currency union. Then he stresses, that small open economies are not strong enough to have their own currencies. Also the fact, that a competition would arise on the banking sector is completely wrong. A currency union with Australia has no influence on the growth of New Zealand's economy, Brash adds. A final myth is, that New Zealand should follow the path of pooling economical forces in currency unions.

Advantages of the currency union:

Elimination of transaction costs: Especially for small open economies, the exchange rate changes can have an important influence on prices. The elimination of costs of exchanging into the domestic currency is the most visible effect of a monetary union, with the cost savings being proportional to the number of transactions conducted in foreign currency. This could also influence the trade and stimulate the open competition. In principle, the costs involved in exchanging different currencies constitute a net dead-weight loss for a nation as a whole. *Reduction of the interest rates*: For Australia and New Zealand, the monetary union could be a possible solution, as the two economies share similar monetary policy frameworks, are at a similar stage of development, and the two currencies are highly correlated already. Legal and institutional frameworks are also similar. Brash also calls the adjusted interest rates in the long-term period another aspect of monetary integration. In the short-term the New Zealand interest rates are on a higher level than those in Australia. An adoption of the Australian dollar and a creation of a new monetary union would also mean a reduction of the average interest rates of NZ. In both cases, whether the integration to the U.S. dollar, or to the Australian dollar, New Zealand would prevent to be liable to the risk premium which savers currently demand for holding New Zealand dollar assets. But this union will also avert any possibility of New Zealand's interest rates to fall under an average level of those in Australia or the U.S. As history shows, there were times, in which the interest rates of New Zealand were below those of the USA or Australia. Perhaps it could be regarded as an extremely rare case, but it has to be considered. New Zealand's interest rates have been so high, because of high-inflation expectations and several decades of high inflation. Brash calls possible reasons for low interest rates: Inflation must be kept under control and confidence to the financial markets. *Stimulate trade within the union.* Brash mentions that as a result of the reduction of the interest rates, only the trade within the member states of the currency union would be stimulated, but he also emphasises, that this is a very important part of the New Zealand trade and especially small companies check the competitiveness of their products,until they enter international markets.

Disadvantages of the currency union:

Brash calls the *loss of an independent monetary policy* and the effect of circumstances beyond out of control *to influence the own inflation rate* the major disadvantages. In this case it does not matter, if there would be a new currency union or simply dollarization. Nevertheless, Brash argues in support of creating the union with Australia, as this would not have such far reaching effects on the loss of New Zealand's influence on monetary policy. However, a monetary union affects in any case both the short and the long run. In the short run, the macroeconomic stabilisation function can be valuable, especially once it is recognised that the fiscal policy instrument is blunter and more politically sensitive. In the long run, the main difficulty lies with inflation. New Zealand applies inflation targeting to achieve its economic proposals (Bernanke, Laubach, Mishkin, Posen, 2001, p.86) The central feature of an inflation-targeting framework is that the inflation target is the primary objective for monetary policy, that concentrates on stabilizing inflation rates. This feature differentiates an inflation-targeting framework from one in which the central bank simply announces a forecast for inflation that it would like to achieve. How successful this works, can be shown in the following graphics: Since introduction of inflation-targeting in 1989, the inflation rates dropped. (Kyongwook, Jung, Shambora, 2003, p.2)

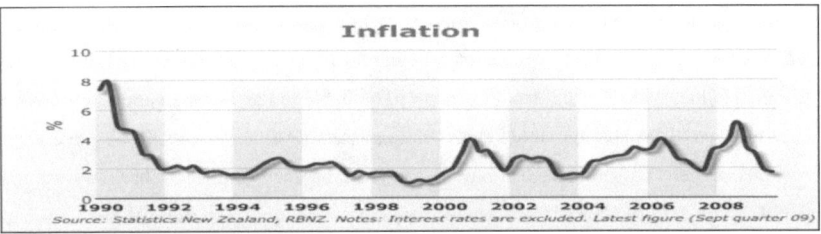

Another effect is the possibility of asymmetric shocks: Sustainable and unexpected economical impulses on the supply side or the demand side of the market. But also financial impulses could trigger asymmetric price-production or labour shocks in the affected countries. Price increase of natural resources will not only affect exporters and importers, but also countries within a monetary union. An example could bet the substitution of other resources. Within a system of flexible foreign exchange rates, this shock would be cushioned by a change of the nominal exchange rates. Brash gives an example, as he explains the situation of Argentina, after joining the U.S. dollar system. For Argentina, this had far reaching economic consequences. They had a prolonged time of recession, longer than any other Latin-American country. The U.S dollar was too closely linked to the U.S currency. The level, on which the currency was lifted, took no account of the relation to the country and its economic possibilities. Endangerments could be an over-heating national economy.

Digression: The Taylor rule and its relevance to New Zealand monetary policy in independence: Basics: The Taylor rule says that short-term interest rates should be "neutral" on average, so that the central bank does not cause persistent inflationary or disinflationary pressures, and that interest rates should be adjusted in response to the current state of the economy. If demand is high relative to productive capacity, short-term interest rates should be raised, and if inflation is above target, interest rates should be raised. Conversely, if the

4

economy is operating below its capacity, or inflation is running below the target inflation rate, the Taylor rule suggests that short-term interest rates should be reduced.

The Taylor rule is a useful part of the Reserve Bank's analytical toolbox. It provides a framework for checking our thinking on the appropriate level for the OCR. As the subject of much recent research, the Taylor rule seems to be a robust way of setting monetary policy, though it is unlikely to be optimal in all circumstances. Within a monetary union, New Zealand would lose this established tool of monetary policy. (Plantier, Scrimgeour, Bulletin Vol. 65 No. 1, p.5)

Conclusion:

First of all: there is equilibrium in the pros and cons. A clear solution is not formulated by D. Brash. Although there are some interesting aspects of creating a new currency system in New Zealand, Brash exemplifies Canada to show, that a successful interrelation in trade between Canada and the U.S. does not depend on a common currency. Nearly 80 of Canada's trade is done with the USA. Another aspect is the "syndicate" of the business community, which comes out in favour of a currency union with Australia. But this are more political facets, not based on economical principles. But it is no question of the advantages to vanquish currency uncertainty, but a question of the economical costs. Brash therefore illustrates the case of falling export prices: with a NZD, the currency will certainly fall. This has an effect to the whole currency area. Less imports will be bought. But without the NZD, there will be the risk, that the currency will not adjust to the new level and the export level will have reduced.

Finally, Brash adds, that a currency union would not ensure a substantially faster New Zealand growth. There is no substitute to compensate domestic policies that promote stronger productivity growth. It is not an issue which should be decided in haste. And it is not an issue on which the Reserve Bank will be taking sides.

In my opinion, there are two possible solutions: First, a monetary union with Australia and a new currency system with an independent central bank, or New Zealand to keep its independent currency. Afterwards, I will analyse the benefits of the two strategies. *Currency unions* represent the highest level of monetary integration. In any case, we will find pros and cons, but most important in terms of globalization, is the economical integration and the development of international markets. This is always more easy, if there is a steady currency system. Some aspects: "One currency-one market": this means the political integration for one thing and the economical alliance for another thing. The EU shows, economical consolidation leads the way to a new level of development of markets with a strong and independent central bank. Because of the abolition of the risk that currency valorisations and devaluations might interfere efficient markets, as eliminating the exchange rate through the outright adoption of another currency would eradicate the potential for a currency crisis. The disappearance of exchange risks also gives companies planning security and helps emerging markets to grow. This is a very strong argument for companies to enter new markets and to foster an economic merging especially in New Zealand, as its national economic is very export-oriented, because New Zealand is a country with limited internal resources. Additional, the intra-trans-Australian trade will be accelerated. Economically regarded, the introduction of a new type of supranational monetary policy, which is not influenced by political adverse influences, will force the world-wide integration of this trans-Australian union. But another strategy would be *to keep independence*. Especially the inflation targeting policy is a very important argument. Some basics: Inflation targeting is a monetary policy framework in which central banks set an inflation rate target and make use of all available policy instruments to attain the goal. New Zealand is an inflation targeting pioneer and the first country to adopt inflation targeting policy. New Zealand, which had experienced high and volatile inflation in the past, has been successful in bringing inflation in line with other OECD countries by adopting inflation targeting. Inflation has fallen throughout the developed world in the last decade[1] but, as indicated, inflation in New Zealand not only fell in absolute terms, it fell relative to inflation in other developed countries. What this all amounts to be that there is no final conclusion, but a consideration. New Zealand and Australia are referring to their economical framework nearly similar, so a currency union would be the most efficient way to summarise all the pros and cons, as the European convergence criteria show, that similar economical efficiency is most important for a efficient monetary union.

List of literature:

1) Brash, Donald T. (2000): "The pros and cons of currency union: A Reserve Bank perspective"
Online: www.rbnz.govt.nz/research/bulletin/1997_2001/2000jun63_2brash22may.pdf
Date of access: October 17, 2009

2) Grimes, Arthur / Holmes, Frank (2000): "An ANZAC Dollar? Currency Union and Business Development" Wellington: Institute of Policy Studies

3) Bernanke, Ben S. / Laubach, Thomas / Mishkin, Frederic S. / Posen, Adam S. (1999): "Inflation targeting: lessons from the international experience", Princeton University Press

4) Kyongwook, Choi / Jung, Chulho / Shambora, William (2003) "Macroeconomic Effects of Inflation Targeting Policy in New Zealand." Economics Bulletin, Vol. 5 No. 17

5) Plantier, Chris / Scrimgeour, Dean "The Taylor rule and its relevance to New Zealand monetary policy" Economics Department of the Reserve bank of New Zealand Bulletin Vol. 65 No. 1